IMAGES
of America

WEST VIRGINIA IN
THE CIVIL WAR

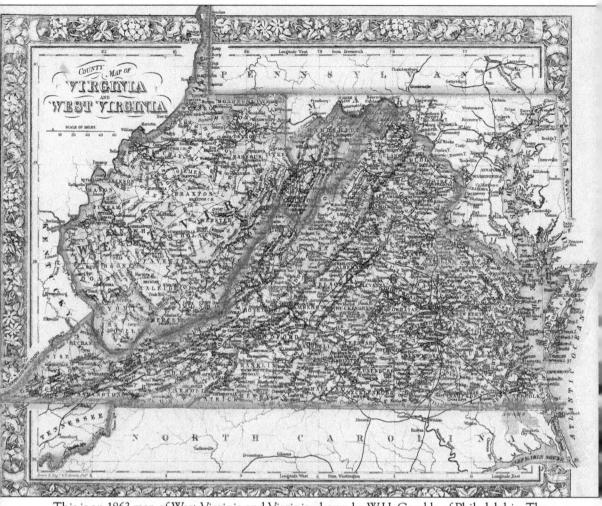

This is an 1863 map of West Virginia and Virginia, drawn by W.H. Gamble of Philadelphia. The eastern panhandle is missing the counties of Berkeley and Jefferson. These two counties were included in West Virginia only because the Baltimore & Ohio Railroad ran through them. This may be the first map of West Virginia published after it attained statehood. (Author's collection.)

ON THE COVER: This is a 1920s photograph of members of the Grand Army of the Republic, Reno Post. The veterans are in front of the train station in Grafton. The man on the right may be one of the veterans' sons, as he is wearing a Son of Union Veterans medal. (Author's collection.)

IMAGES
of America

WEST VIRGINIA IN
THE CIVIL WAR

Richard A. Wolfe

ARCADIA
PUBLISHING

Published by Arcadia Publishing
Charleston, South Carolina

Library of Congress Control Number: 2013936611

For all general information, please contact Arcadia Publishing:
Telephone 843-853-2070
Fax 843-853-0044
E-mail sales@arcadiapublishing.com
For customer service and orders:
Toll-Free 1-888-313-2665

Visit us on the Internet at www.arcadiapublishing.com

To my parents, Wanda Perrine Wolfe and the late Clifford A. Wolfe. As part of the generation that lived through the Depression and fought World War II, they taught me many important lessons of life. They taught me to love and respect this nation.

CONTENTS

ACKNOWLEDGMENTS

Over the years, four individuals have helped me in researching West Virginia's role in the Civil War. To Terry Lowry, Steve Cunningham, Hunter Lesser, and Mark Snell, I owe a great deal of thanks. The following very generous people assisted me in putting this book together: Carol Schweiker, Jon-Erik Gilot, Lemeul Muniz, Richard "Dick" Duez, Dora Grub, Roger Ware, Mike Chancey, Bekah Karelis, Donald Rice, Mike Smith, Margarette Brennan, Daniel Toomey, Darryl DeGripp, John Allen, Travis Henline, Joe Geiger, Debra Basham, Jane Rissier, Shannon Proud, Todd Funkhouser, Tom White, and Al Pjack. Thank you.

The following organizations provided me with assistance in putting in this book together: Rich Mountain Battlefield Foundation, Harrison County Historic Society, Jefferson County Museum, Berkeley County Historical Society, Fort Mill Ridge Foundation, West Virginia State Archives, Baltimore & Ohio Railroad Museum, George Tyler Moore Center for the Study of the Civil War, Marion County Historical Society, Hanger, Inc., and Beverly Heritage Center.

I want to thank my publisher, Rebekah Collinsworth, of Arcadia Publishing, for her valuable assistance.

Foremost, I want to thank Belinda Moore for her support and understanding. She has always been patient during our visits to the historic sites in West Virginia.

Unless otherwise noted, all images are from my collection or were photographed by me.

INTRODUCTION

Without the Civil War, the state of West Virginia would not exist. The major cause of the war was the expansion of slavery. But the issue of slavery had nothing to do with western counties separating from the mother state of Virginia. There was no mention of slavery during the First and Second Wheeling Conventions. When West Virginia entered the Union as a slave state, many of the southern counties were under Confederate control. Also, 40 percent of the population of West Virginia voted for secession, with many citizens serving in the Confederate army. Was the birth of West Virginia legal, or just expedient? West Virginia's existence depended on the survival of the Union as a whole. A Union supporter said of the state, "Born of the Rebellion," while a former Confederate called the state "The Bastard Child of Political Rape." The creation of West Virginia was unique, and it makes for a fascinating and intriguing story.

Before the American Revolution, there was a movement in 1774 to create a 14th colony. Called Vandalia, it would encompass much of West Virginia and part of Kentucky. It would include land from the Allegheny Mountains to the Ohio River. The War of Independence, however, ended the formation of Vandalia.

Sectional conflict had existed in Virginia politics since the Revolutionary War. Virginia was divided into four sections: Tidewater, Piedmont, the Valley, and Trans-Allegheny. The Tidewater and Piedmont sections were the counties east of the Blue Ridge Mountains. These sections had a large slave population. The issues of taxation, internal improvements, and political apportionment divided the sections. Tidewater and Piedmont were favored over the Valley and Trans-Allegheny sections, despite the almost evenly split white populations. Tidewater and Piedmont counties had a white population of 362,745, and the Valley and Trans-Allegheny sections had 319,518. About one-third of the Virginia population was slaves, most residing in Tidewater and Piedmont. The eastern sections had 68 convention delegates to the western sections' 28. The west lost before the convention even started. Until the 1830s, it was the Valley and Trans-Allegheny regions that were not treated fairly. In the 1830s, however, the increase of slaves into the valley, the addition of four representatives, and internal improvements swayed the Valley region into abandoning its support of the Trans-Allegheny region. As the Civil War approached, it was evident that not all of what is now West Virginia was pro-Union. The counties that bordered the Ohio River, Pennsylvania, and the Baltimore & Ohio Railroad were pro-Union. The majority of the counties preferred not to pick sides. The Trans-Allegheny section was also divided; the northwestern portion was against secession, and the southwestern counties voted for secession. West Virginia was the most divided state during the Civil War.

The presidential election of November 6, 1860, sent the Union into crisis. The victory by Abraham Lincoln, who was against allowing slavery to expand into the territories and free states, was seen as threatening in the South. The Southern slaveholding states saw their political power eroding in favor of the Northern states. On December 20, 1860, South Carolina seceded. It sent agents to the other Southern states, urging them to follow.

After the election of Lincoln, Virginia governor John Letcher called for an extra session of the general assembly to meet on January 8, 1861. It was clear that the reason for this session was to discuss secession. The only pro-Lincoln paper in Virginia, the *Wheeling Intelligencer*, printed a quote from Tyler County: "We are for secession at once, and let the Blue Ridge of mountains be the line." The *Intelligencer* editor added, "Let the South Carolina politicians in our midst put that in their pipes." Archibald Campbell, the editor of the *Wheeling Intelligencer*, did as much to push statehood as any politician. His newspaper was the only one in the South to support Lincoln for president. During the war, the *Intelligencer* was distributed to soldiers via the B&O Railroad. It printed soldiers' letters and was a very strong supporter of West Virginia statehood.

The Virginia General Assembly declared that, if the North and South failed to reach a compromise, Virginia would unite with the slaveholding states. It then called for the election of delegates for a secession convention to meet in Richmond on February 13, 1861. In the early days of the convention, it appeared that Virginia would stay in the Union.

On April 12, the Confederates fired on Fort Sumter, and on April 15, President Lincoln called for 75,000 militiamen to be activated into service for three months. Virginia's allotment was three regiments, but Governor Letcher refused to honor the request. The convention reacted; on the morning of April 17, ex-governor Henry Wise addressed the delegates. He started by drawing a pistol from his coat and informing them that he had sent Virginia troops to seize the federal arsenal at Harpers Ferry and the US Navy yard at Norfolk. In a loud and bellicose voice, Wise said that Virginia was taking control of every square foot of federal property within its borders. By the end of the day, the convention voted, 88 to 55, to send the ordinance of secession to the voters. That did not change the fact that federal property had been illegally seized before the citizens of Virginia voted on secession.

The northwestern delegates recognized the warning signs. Some, like John S. Carlile, quickly left Richmond, while others, fearing for their safety, requested passes from the governor. Carlile departed the convention on April 19 for Clarksburg. He quickly called for a meeting at the Harrison County Court House. At a mass meeting, the Clarksburg Resolutions were passed. This would lead to the First Wheeling Convention.

On May 13, 1861, delegates from 27 western Virginia counties met in Wheeling for what is referred to as the First Wheeling Convention. Carlile proposed immediate separation from Virginia to form the state of New Virginia. At this convention, nothing was resolved because the citizens had not voted on the secession ordinance. The delegates firmly resolved to form a provisional state government should the Virginia voters pick secession.

On May 23, 1861, Virginia voted to leave the Union. The ordinance of secession received 125,950 yes votes and 20,373 votes against. An overwhelming majority of Virginians voted for secession, but the majority of those in the northwestern counties voted against it.

During this time, Virginia was readying for war. On April 27, Col. Thomas J. Jackson was placed in command at Harpers Ferry, and on May 14, Col. George Porterfield arrived in Grafton, just 100 railroad miles from Wheeling. Porterfield was to recruit and take charge of Confederate troops in western Virginia. Discovering that Grafton was a pro-Union town, he went to Fetterman and found Capt. W.P. Thompson with his Company of Marion Guards. The Union side was not idle. On May 10, the first company of the 1st Virginia (Federal) Infantry was mustered at Wheeling. On May 13, Gen. George B. McClellan assumed command of the Department of the Ohio, which included portions of western Virginia.

The Second Wheeling Convention started on June 11, 1861, in Washington Hall but was moved to the US Custom House on June 13. There were 88 delegates from 32 counties. On June 20, the Restored Government of Virginia was established, and Francis H. Pierpont was elected governor. On July 13, John Carlile and Waitman T. Willey were seated as US senators from the state of Virginia. A general assembly was established. A proposal for a new 39-county state named Kanawha was passed, and a date for a constitutional convention was set. All of this was accomplished between June 11 and August 21, when the Second Wheeling Convention adjourned.

The Confederates in Grafton feared that Union troops in Wheeling were planning an attack on their camp. On May 25, Confederates from their camp at Grafton were sent to burn railroad bridges. Lt. Col. William J. Willey, half-brother of Waitman T. Willey, burnt two B&O bridges that crossed Buffalo Creek, between Mannington and Farmington. This destruction of the B&O Railroad set in motion the invasion of northwestern Virginia by Federal troops. Col. Benjamin F. Kelley communicated the destruction of the bridges to General McClellan. On May 27, Kelley moved by train from Wheeling with the objective of protecting the railroad and the rights of the people. McClellan's Ohio and Indiana soldiers, who were following on the railroad from Wheeling and Parkersburg, supported Kelley. The Union forces under Kelley attacked the Confederate forces at Philippi on June 3. Now, thousands of Federal troops entered Virginia. The Union forces remained on the offensive, winning battles at Laurel Hill and Rich Mountain and killing Confederate general Robert S. Garnett at Corrick Ford. McClellan stationed troops along the vital B&O Railroad to protect it from Confederate destruction. This was to be the first campaign of the Civil War.

The proposal for a new state was put before the voters. On October 24, 1861, with most of northwestern Virginia behind Federal lines, residents of 41 counties voted for the dismemberment of Virginia. Of the 50,000 eligible voters, only 37 percent cast ballots. More than 18,000 favored a new state, with fewer than 800 voting in the negative.

A constitutional convention was set for November 26, 1861, in Wheeling. Besides writing a constitution for a new state, other questions required answers. What name would the new state have? New Virginia, Western Virginia, Allegheny, Kanawha, or West Virginia? What would the boundaries be? How many counties would be included? What of the slavery issue?

On February 18, 1862, the convention approved the constitution for the new state of West Virginia. The constitution addressed issues that had been longtime complaints by the Virginians of the west: representation in both houses of the legislature was based on white population, universal white male suffrage over the age of 21, and a free school system. The citizens approved the constitution, more than 18,000 in favor versus 514 against. During this time, the Restored Government of Virginia, led by Governor Pierpont, was in full operation, operating a government and a war. The approval of the Restored Government of Virginia was required due to the provisions in the US Constitution. The request for a new state was submitted to the Restored Government of Virginia for approval, which was received on May 13, 1862. The final agreement for the size of the state was 50 counties. The desire to keep the B&O Railroad in Union control resulted in Jefferson and Berkeley Counties being included. Later, Governor Pierpont moved the government to Alexandria and, after the war, to Richmond.

On May 29, 1862, Waitman Willey formally introduced a new state petition to the US Senate. Senator Carlile was given the task of writing the bill. He rewrote it to add an additional 15 counties. This anti-secession, pro-dismemberment bill was also pro-slavery. That may be the answer to why Carlile tried to defeat West Virginia statehood. Senator Willey stepped forward to save West Virginia statehood. The question of allowing a slave state to enter the Union was in the forefront. The "Willey Amendment" would allow for the gradual emancipation of slaves in the new state. On July 14, 1862, the amended statehood bill passed the US Senate by a vote of 23 to 17.

After the defeat of Gen. Robert S. Garnett's forces at Rich Mountain and his death at Corrick Ford, Gen. Henry Wise being thrown out of the Kanawha Valley, and Gen. Robert E. Lee's failure in the mountains, western Virginia was no longer in danger of falling under Confederate control. The area alongside and north of the B&O Railroad was in Union control. Major battles were ending in 1861, but the bitter warfare did not. There were cavalry raids, fights for the Kanawha Valley, and protection of the B&O. Guerrilla warfare became a big part of the fighting.

On December 21, President Lincoln received the West Virginia statehood bill and asked his cabinet for advice. Half of the cabinet favored admission of West Virginia, and half opposed it. On December 31, 1862, the president signed the bill, giving these remarks: "The division of the State is dreaded as a precedent. But a measure made expedient by war is no precedent for times of peace. It is said that the admission of West Virginia is secession and tolerated only because it is our secession. Well, if we call it by that name there is still difference enough between secession against the Constitution and secession in favor of the Constitution. I believe the admission of West Virginia into the Union is expedient."

In February 1863, the West Virginia Constitutional Convention reconvened and adopted the Willey Amendment. On March 26, 1863, the voters approved the West Virginia Constitution with the emancipation amendment. On April 20, President Lincoln signed the West Virginia statehood bill to take effect in 60 days. On April 23, Confederate generals William Jones and John Imboden launched a destructive raid through the soon-to-be new state, focusing on the railroad. While disruptive, the raid had no impact on West Virginia statehood. On May 28, the voters elected Arthur I. Boreman the first governor of West Virginia. On June 20, 1863, West Virginia became the 35th state in the Union.

One

1859

JOHN BROWN'S RAID

John Brown's raid on Harpers Ferry to destroy the institution of slavery did not start the Civil War, but most historians believe that it played a significant role. Brown was a fiery abolitionist who believed in action and not words. Influential abolitionists supported Brown financially, including Gerritt Smith, Samuel Gridley Howe, Theodore Parker, George Luther Stearns, Franklin Sanborn, and Thomas Wentworth Higginson. They were known as the Secret Six.

Brown briefly outlined his plans to Frederick Douglass. He would capture weapons at Harpers Ferry and move into the Allegheny Mountains, using the mountains as a fortress and helping slaves escape to Canada. He believed that the slaveholders would finally give up the practice.

In July 1859, Brown visited Harpers Ferry and, soon afterward, rented the Kennedy farm near the ferry in Maryland. Assuming the name Isaac Smith, Brown gave the appearance of a working farmer.

On October 16, 1859, under the cover of darkness, Brown and 18 of his raiders departed from the Kennedy farm and moved toward Harpers Ferry. They crossed over the bridge, cut the telegraph line, secured the second bridge into Harpers Ferry, and seized the US Arsenal on Hall's Island. Brown sent other members of his party to take hostages. Slave owners Lewis Washington and John Allstadt were taken hostage and their slaves freed. Lewis Washington was the great-grandnephew of George Washington.

On October 17, 1859, at around 1:30 a.m., a B&O train was stopped at the bridge. Heyward Shepherd, a free African American and a railroad employee, investigated. He ignored demands to halt and was mortally wounded, ironically becoming the first death of the raid.

Local farmers and townspeople surrounded the armory. The local militia captured the bridge across the Potomac River, cutting off the raiders' escape route. Brown's men took refuge in the fire engine house, taking nine hostages. Marines from the Washington Navy Yard soon arrived and quickly captured Brown and put down the insurrection. Brown faced charges of treason and was hanged. This was not the end of John Brown. Union soldiers would sing of John Brown's body and his soul.

John Brown was a "fire-breathing" abolitionist who used violence to fight slavery. He commanded antislavery factions in Kansas. In 1856, he and his men killed five pro-slavery supporters at Pottawatomie. He left "Bleeding Kansas" and, in 1859, conducted an unsuccessful raid on the federal armory at Harpers Ferry.

The industrial town of Harpers Ferry is located at the confluence of the Potomac and Shenandoah Rivers. In 1799, the US government established an arsenal and armory there. In the early 1830s, the town saw the B&O Railroad arrive. This picturesque town was the object of John Brown's raid in October 1859.

Shown here is the fire engine house at Harpers Ferry. On October 16, 1859, John Brown and a small army of men launched a raid to capture weapons and to arm slaves, with the goal of forming a new government. His group included 16 white men, 3 free blacks, 1 freed slave, and 1 fugitive slave. Brown's men took a number of hostages.

This east-facing photograph of Harpers Ferry shows Shenandoah Street. At the end of the street, it intersects with Potomac Street, where the US Armory and engine house were located. As the sun came up on October 17, citizens started shooting at the raiders. The local militia arrived and surrounded the raiders. The streets of Harpers Ferry were filled with soldiers and spectators.

Col. Robert E. Lee was directed to Harpers Ferry to command the Marines to quell Brown's insurrection. Lee, in civilian clothes and accompanied by Lt. J.E.B. Stuart, left Washington sometime after the Marines. Lee met his forces, commanded by Lt. Israel Greene, at Sandy Hook, Maryland. The Marines marched to Harpers Ferry and took charge of the armory area around the engine house. Lee directed Stuart to demand Brown's surrender.

The Marines tried to batter down the door with sledgehammers. Then they used a ladder as a battering ram. The second blow created a hole, through which Lieutenant Greene rushed in. Greene, wielding a light sword, smashed Brown on the head with all his strength. Then he thrust the sword into Brown's chest. The light sword bent double. Very quickly, the Marines captured the raiders and freed the hostages.

Pvt. Luke Quinn was the only Marine killed in the assault on the engine house. He was the second Marine to enter after Lieutenant Greene. John Brown had just reloaded his carbine and fired, striking Quinn in the abdomen. The Irish immigrant died soon after. He was buried in the Catholic Cemetery overlooking the water gap at Harpers Ferry.

The engine house became a symbol of John Brown's raid and the fight for freedom. Over the years, the facility became known of John Brown's Fort. In 1893, it was transported to Chicago for the World's Columbian Exposition, then to the Murphy farm near Harpers Ferry, and then to the campus of Storer College. The structure was moved many times until arriving at its present location, 150 feet from its original spot, in 1968.

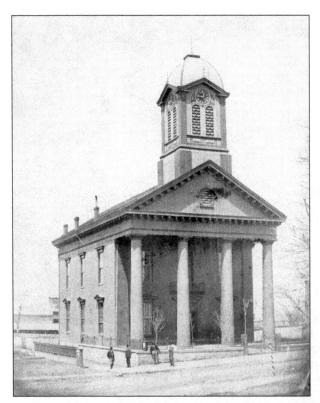

The 1836 Jefferson County Court House in Charles Town was the site of John Brown's trial. Brown was arraigned on October 25, 1859. On the 26th, the charges were announced: treason against the Commonwealth of Virginia, inciting slaves to rebel, and the murders of George Turner, Fontaine Beckham, Thomas Boerly, Heyward Shepherd, and Luke Quinn.

Richard Parker was the circuit judge for the city of Winchester and the counties of Jefferson and Frederick. This Winchester resident was determined that Brown receive a fair trial. Andrew Hunter, a prominent Jefferson County attorney and congressman, served as the prosecuting attorney, assisted by Charles Harding. A number of lawyers were assigned to defend Brown, but they declined, for a variety of reasons.

The trial began on October 26, 1859. Brown's lawyers were Hiram Griswold, Samuel Chilton, and George Hoyt. Brown, suffering from his wounds, was carried to and from the jail. He had to lie on a cot in the courtroom. On October 31, after only 45 minutes of deliberation, the verdict of guilty on all counts was delivered. Brown was sentenced to hang on December 2, 1859.

Brown was incarcerated in the Charles Town jail during and after the trial. Concerns arose that there would be an attempt to free Brown. Charles Town was heavily guarded with soldiers and was under martial law. Brown received several visitors, and many letters were sent to Governor Wise asking to spare Brown's life.

The bearded John Brown was hanged on December 2, 1859. Before his execution, he wrote the following prediction: "Charlestown, Va. 2 December 1859. I John Brown am now quite certain that the crimes of this guilty land will never be purged away but with blood. I had, as I now think, vainly flattered myself that without very much bloodshed it might be done."

John Brown's body was taken to the family farm in North Elba, New York, for burial. Over time, 11 of the raiders were buried there. Did John Brown start the Civil War? Fredrick Douglass said, "It was not Carolina, but Virginia, not Fort Sumter, but Harpers Ferry, not Major Anderson but John Brown who began the war that ended slavery and made this a free republic."

Two

1860–1861

UNION OR DISUNION

On November 6, 1860, Abraham Lincoln was elected president of the United States. He received no electoral votes from the Southern states. As the slaveholding states talked secession, the western Virginia counties held pro-Union meetings. One of the first was in Clarksburg on November 24 to oppose the ordinance of secession passed by South Carolina. Before Lincoln's inauguration, South Carolina seceded. All eyes turned to Virginia, which had the largest slave population—474,464 slaves, 16,401 of who were in the counties that became West Virginia.

After Virginia voted to secede, delegates met in Wheeling to form a loyal government and to seek a process to establish a state independent of Virginia. Gov. Francis Pierpont secured funds for the new government. Even though these men were loyal to the Union, they were considered traitors to the Confederate State of Virginia.

The Baltimore & Ohio Railroad had to remain in Union hands. The Restored Government of Virginia started recruiting men for the army. At the same time, Confederates were recruiting the same men to the Southern cause. The military quotas for Pennsylvania and Ohio were filled quickly, so some men came to Virginia to enlist. The 2nd West Virginia Cavalry, for example, was composed mostly of men from Ohio. They had tried to enter service as a cavalry unit in Ohio, but the governor was not enlisting cavalry units. These men crossed the river and became the 2nd Cavalry. They provided gallant service from September 1861 until Appomattox.

By August 1861, most of the counties around the railroad or along the Ohio River were safely in Union control. The large number of Union troops along the B&O, mostly from Ohio and Indiana, convinced many of the citizens to support the Union. This military-controlled buffer also gave the politicians in Wheeling a sense of safety.

The first year of the war saw West Virginia on the road to statehood. Confederate general Henry Wise sent a telegraph to Richmond in September 1861: "The Kanawha Valley is wholly traitorous. . . . You cannot persuade these people that Virginia can or ever will reconquer the northwest."

On November 6, 1860, Abraham Lincoln was elected the 16th president of the United States, with only 39.8 percent of the popular vote. He received only 1,402 votes from the counties that became West Virginia. Lincoln was sworn in on March 4, 1861. On April 12, Confederate troops fired on Union-held Fort Sumter in Charleston, South Carolina. On April 14, Lincoln issued a call for 75,000 militiamen to serve for 90 days. (Courtesy Library of Congress.)

This plaque, located in the Harrison County Court House, marks the site of the Union meeting held by John S. Carlile that produced the Clarksburg Resolutions. The resolutions called for a convention in Wheeling, known as the First Wheeling Convention. This meeting, attended by nearly 1,200 citizens, was held on April 22, 1861, just days after the Virginia Secession Convention voted to secede and join the slaveholding Confederacy.

THIS TABLET IS ERECTED TO KEEP BEFORE FUTURE GENERATIONS THE VIRTUES AND COURAGE OF THE PEOPLE OF HARRISON COUNTY, WHO, AT A TIME OF GREAT CIVIL COMMOTION, ASSEMBLED IN MASS MEETING ON THE 22ND DAY OF APRIL, 1861, IN THE COURT HOUSE THEN OCCUPYING THIS SPOT, AND TOOK ACTION IN THE ADOPTION OF RESOLUTIONS, CALLING ON THE PEOPLE OF NORTH WESTERN VIRGINIA, TO APPOINT DELEGATES TO MEET IN CONVENTION AT WHEELING ON THE 13TH DAY OF MAY, FOLLOWING, TO CONSULT AND DETERMINE WHAT ACTION SHOULD BE TAKEN IN THE EMERGENCY CONFRONTING THEM.
THIS PROCEEDING WAS THE INITIAL MOVEMENT THAT FINALLY RESULTED IN THE CREATION OF THE STATE OF WEST VIRGINIA FROM THE TERRITORY OF THE STATE OF VIRGINIA.
THE MEETING WAS PRESIDED OVER BY JOHN HURSEY WITH JOHN W. HARRIS AS SECRETARY.
THE FOLLOWING DELEGATES WERE APPOINTED TO THE WHEELING CONVENTION
JOHN S. CARLILE
WALDO P. GOFF
JOHN J. DAVIS
THOMAS L. MOORE
SOLOMON S. FLEMING
LOT BOWEN
WILLIAM DUNKIN
WILLIAM E. LYON
FELIX S. STURM
BENJAMIN F. SHUTTLEWORTH
JAMES LYNCH
1914

Washington Hall in Wheeling was the site of the First Wheeling Convention, on May 13, 1861. This meeting had delegates from 27 western Virginia counties. John S. Carlile called for the immediate separation from Virginia to form the state of New Virginia. Waitman T. Willey called it treason not only against Virginia, but also against the US Constitution. The convention would adjourn until after the secession vote. (Courtesy Bekah Karelis.)

William H. Carothers, later an adviser to Governor Pierpont, was instrumental in securing rifles for the 1st Virginia Infantry. The federal government would not send weapons to Virginia, despite the fact that a Union regiment was being formed. Carothers and Campbell Tarr arranged with Massachusetts governor John Curtin for rifles to be sent to Wheeling.

The fairgrounds on Wheeling Island became the site of the camp for Union companies. This was in support of President Lincoln's call for three regiments of 90-day volunteers to suppress the rebellious South. On May 16, men moved across the suspension bridge to the island, setting up Camp Carlile. These volunteers became the 1st Virginia (Federal) Infantry. (Courtesy Diocese of Wheeling-Charleston Archives.)

The marketplace in Wheeling, Center Market, was the site of many meetings. The Union companies adopted names. The Henry Clay Guards, accompanied by the Iron Guards and the Rough and Ready Rifles, marched to the market to receive a flag from the citizens of Wheeling. The men, not yet outfitted with uniforms, looked more like a mob. The only favorable sights were the glittering bayonets, bright rifles, and music playing. (Courtesy Diocese of Wheeling-Charleston Archives.)

The Wheeling waterfront was very active. Steamboats moved troops and supplies across the Ohio River, destined for the B&O Railroad in support of the war effort against the Confederacy. On the evening of May 20, the 1st Virginia experienced its first causality. The Hancock Guards were en route to Wheeling on the steamer *S.C. Baker* when Thomas J. Baker fell off and drowned.

This is a marker to the first soldier killed in the Civil War. On the night of May 22, Lt. Daniel Wilson and Pvt. Thornsberry Bailey Brown walked toward the Confederate camp at Fetterman. They approached Confederate pickets Daniel Knight and George Glenn. The pickets ordered the Union soldiers to stop. They did not stop, and Private Brown fired at the pickets, hitting Knight on the ear. Knight shot back, killing Brown instantly.

Benjamin Franklin Kelley lived most of his adult life in Wheeling. He commanded the first
Union regiment formed in a Southern state during the Civil War. On May 27, Kelley moved from
Wheeling toward Grafton. In the first battle of the war, he became one of the first Union officers
wounded. Kelley recovered from his wound, was appointed brigadier general, and was assigned to
protect the Baltimore & Ohio Railroad.

The scene of the courtroom during the Second Wheeling Convention is seen here in a *Harper's Weekly* sketch. After the citizens of Virginia voted to secede on May 23, 1861, pro-Union delegates from western Virginia were selected for a convention. On June 11, 1861, a meeting was held involving 88 delegates from 32 western Virginia counties to establish a Restored Government of Virginia.

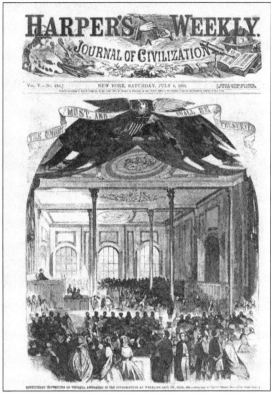

Francis H. Pierpont, a lawyer from Fairmont, was elected the governor of the Restored Government of Virginia at the Second Wheeling Convention. He received death threats for being a part of the Union Virginia government. He is called the "Father of West Virginia," but he never served as governor of the state. In 1863, he moved the Virginia government to Alexandria and then to Richmond after the war, serving as governor until 1869. (Courtesy Hunter Lesser.)

The Grafton Hotel and railroad station sat at the junction of the B&O and the Northwest Virginia Railroads. From here, the B&O goes northwest to Wheeling and the Northwest Virginia travels west to Parkersburg on the Ohio River. The Battle of Philippi was planned in this hotel, and the wounded Colonel Kelley was brought here after the battle.

On May 27, 1861, the invasion of western Virginia by Federal forces started. Gen. George B. McClellan directed this crossing of the Ohio River both at Wheeling and, as this sketch depicts, at Parkersburg. The wharf at Parkersburg was filled with soldiers and war supplies that would be moved by rail to Grafton.

Union forces in two columns left Grafton to attack and capture the Confederates at Philippi. Col. Benjamin Franklin Kelley, overall commander of the Virginia forces, was to flank Philippi and block the retreat. Colonel Dumont was to attack the Confederates at dawn. On the morning of June 3, 1861, after a long and rainy march, the Union forces opened fire from the hill overlooking Philippi. The six-pound cannonballs crashed into the Confederate camp. The Union columns, each consisting of 1,500 men, attacked the 750 Confederates. Kelley was leading his 1st Virginia (Federal) Infantry, pursuing the Confederates through the town, when he was shot in the chest. The battle did not last long. It was mockingly called "The Philippi Races." The Confederates retreated to Beverly. There were no deaths in this battle.

James Hanger, a young cavalryman, was in a barn on the morning of June 3, 1861, when a cannonball hit him in the leg. Dr. Robinson of the 16th Ohio Infantry amputated the leg. This was the first amputation of the war. Hanger later developed a moving artificial leg, making walking easier. He would produce artificial limbs for the Confederacy. Hanger, Inc., is in business today producing artificial limbs. (Courtesy Hanger, Inc.)

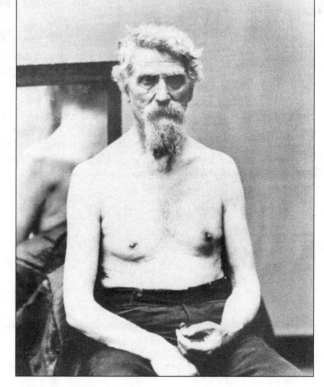

The gunshot that wounded Colonel Kelley entered at his right breast below the clavicle and above the second rib. The ball continued through his body, coming to a rest on the scapula, breaking and bulging it out. Kelley lost much blood. On June 5, he was carried by stretcher 14 miles to Webster Station, then moved by train to Grafton. Doctor Frissell removed the ball later in the year. (Courtesy National Museum of Health & Medicine Armed Forces Institute of Pathology.)

In May 1861, Gen. George McClellan, commander of the Department of the Ohio, ordered troops from Ohio and Indiana into western Virginia to support the Union Virginia forces. He received credit for Union victories at Philippi, Laurel Hill, Rich Mountain, and Corrick Ford. Because of this success and the Union defeat at First Manassas, McClellan was called to Washington to command US forces on July 23, 1861.

Gen. William Rosecrans was an 1842 graduate of West Point. He commanded a brigade in McClellan's army, moving east through western Virginia. The Confederates, commanded by Col. John Pegram, were entrenched on Rich Mountain. Rosecrans presented a plan to McClellan to use a civilian, David Hart, as a guide to flank the Confederates.

This *Harper's Weekly* sketch shows Rosecrans leading a 1,900-men brigade on a flank march over rough terrain and through dense forest to strike the Confederates at the crest of Rich Mountain. David Hart led the Union forces to his family farm, where the Staunton and Parkersburg Turnpike crosses Rich Mountain. After a long march, the Union forces reached the top of the mountain and found it defended by Confederates.

Frederick W. Lander was a volunteer aid to General McClellan who served at the Battle of Philippi. He accompanied Rosecrans's brigade to the top of Rich Mountain. While the brigade was deploying, Lander jumped on a large rock and cursed and shot at the Confederates, stating that he would "beat them like the devil directly." His promotion to brigadier general came in August 1861.

The 310 Confederates, armed with a single six-pound cannon put up a hard fight, but Rosecrans's numbers were too much. During this time, General McClellan, the overall commander, with about 3,000 men, sat paralyzed in front of Camp Garnett. Likewise, on the Confederate side, Lt. Col. John Pegram, with about 1,000 men, stayed at Camp Garnett, not taking action until it was too late.

After the Confederates were defeated at Rich Mountain, Gen. Robert S. Garnett realized that he could not hold Laurel Hill. In the middle of the night, he silently stole out of camp. Union forces were soon in pursuit. It became a running fight in the driving rain. At Corrick Ford, on July 13, 1861, in a rearguard action, Garnett became the first general killed in the Civil War.

When Gen. George McClellan moved across the Rich Mountain battlefield, he brought with him a new technology, the field telegraph. His men laid wires for the telegraph. Before the war, placement of the telegraph in western Virginia was limited to along railroads. The Civil War brought the telegraph to the field and to the battleground. President Lincoln visited the telegraph office for daily news of the war. (Courtesy Library of Congress.)

Shown here are the trenches on Lowndes Hill. During June, General McClellan would send more troops to western Virginia, many being posted along the strategic Baltimore & Ohio Railroad. On June 19, the 8th Indiana Infantry was tasked with building fortifications in Clarksburg. The regiment went to work, digging trenches on Lowndes and Pinnickinnick Hills. The 10th Indiana assisted with this task. By late June, there were eight companies protecting the Clarksburg railroad. (Courtesy Harrison County Historical Society.)

In July 1861, General McClellan went east to command all Federal forces. Gen. William S. Rosecrans assumed command of the Army of Occupation. His headquarters was in Clarksburg where he was coordinating all the troops in western Virginia to include protecting the railroad and fighting Confederates in the Cheat Mountain area. He was planning a campaign to the Kanawha Valley. Rosecrans is shown above conferring with his staff in Clarksburg.

This is an 1861 photograph of Main Street in Clarksburg. Clarksburg, on the Northwest Virginia Railroad, had a telegraph and a very good road network. These things made it perfect as a site for a supply depot. In 1861, Clarksburg supplied the Federal forces in the Cheat Mountain area and in the Kanawha Valley. This was an economic boom to the town. (Courtesy Harrison County Historical Society.)

Construction of the Trans-Allegheny Lunatic Asylum, located in Weston, was started in 1859. Governor Pierpont discovered that Virginia deposited $30,000 in gold to fund the work. He sent Col. Erastus Tyler and his 7th Ohio Infantry to seize the gold. Tyler arrived in Weston on the morning of June 30, 1861, and secured the much-needed funds for the Restored Government of Virginia.

Thomas Jonathan Jackson was born in Clarksburg and raised at Jackson's Mill. He graduated from West Point in the celebrated class of 1846. Jackson was a Mexican War veteran and a professor at Virginia Military Academy. He commanded the armory at Harpers Ferry after Virginia militia seized it on April 18, 1861. US forces abandoned the armory and set it on fire. The Virginia militia put the fire out.

This is an 1860 photograph of the roundhouse at Martinsburg. Armies in the Civil War relied heavily on the railroad. The Baltimore & Ohio Railroad stretched across West Virginia, from Harpers Ferry to Wheeling, a distance of 298 miles. The Union tried to protect the railroad, while the Confederates tried to destroy it. Jackson destroyed this roundhouse and the magnificent Colonnade railroad bridge at Martinsburg in June 1861 before he moved his brigade toward Manassas. Jackson captured railroad engines, cars, and equipment that he then sent south to support the Confederacy. Some historians have referred to this as the Great Train Robbery, while others question the validity of the story. Daniel Carroll Toomey, in his book *The War Came by Train*, provides proof that the event happened. (Courtesy the Baltimore & Ohio Railroad Museum.)

On July 12, 1861, Brig. Gen. Jacob Cox, an Ohio politician, moved Union forces into the Kanawha Valley to confront Confederate forces under Brig. Gen. Henry Wise. Cox suffered a defeat at Scary Creek on July 17, 1861, but did an adequate job of controlling the Kanawha Valley. He was unwittingly helped by Confederate generals Wise and Floyd, who preferred fighting with each other than fighting the Federals.

Erastus Barnard Tyler was engaged in the fur business before the war. He raised the 7th Ohio Infantry and was elected colonel over future president James Garfield. On the morning of August 26, 1861, his regiment was surprised and routed by Gen. John B. Floyd's brigade at Kessler's Cross Lanes. Because Tyler's men were eating breakfast at the outbreak of the fight, this is known as the Battle of Knives and Forks.

John B. Floyd, a governor of Virginia from 1848 to 1852, was secretary of war under President Buchanan. As such, he transferred large numbers of arms to Southern arsenals. On September 10, 1861, Floyd's Confederates battled William Rosecrans's Union forces at Carnifex Ferry. During the night, Floyd moved his command down a rough mountain road and crossed the ferry undetected, leaving control of the area to the Union.

This is a sketch of the Union fort at Cheat Mountain. The fort was built in 1861. The area could be a pleasant place, but at 4,000 feet, it became a cold, miserable place during the wet year of 1861. Substandard uniforms fell apart, leaving the soldiers nearly naked. On August 13, it snowed at the camp. On September 10, Confederate forces under General Lee made an unsuccessful attack on the fort.

Harpers Ferry is seen here in early 1861. This home of the US Armory and Arsenal was all but destroyed during the Civil War. If not for the critical railroad bridge over the Potomac River, the town would have probably been abandoned. The bridge was rebuilt and repaired numerous times. General Jackson blew up the bridge in June 1861 as he left for Manassas and fame as "Stonewall." (Courtesy the Baltimore & Ohio Railroad Museum.)

The Tray Run Viaduct was an iron trestle, 445 feet long and 58 feet high. As General McClellan's army spread through western Virginia, the first priority was protection of the critical Baltimore & Ohio Railroad, which ran from the Ohio River to Baltimore, with a junction to Washington. The only railroad that ran directly from the west to the Union's capital, it was important to the war effort.

38

Joseph Jones Reynolds, a West Point graduate, commanded Union forces at Cheat Mountain. On October 3, 1861, his troops attacked the Confederate camp at Bartow, where the Staunton and Parkersburg Turnpike crosses the Greenbrier River. Unable to dislodge the Confederates, Reynolds retreated from this mostly artillery duel. Michigan's Loomis Battery would use some of the first Parrott Rifles issued to the Union army.

Edward Johnson graduated from West Point in 1838 and served in the Mexican and Seminole Wars. He resigned from the "Old Army" and accepted command of the 12th Georgia Infantry. On December 13, 1861, Colonel Johnson's forces defeated Union troops commanded by Gen. Robert Milroy at Camp Allegheny. The camp was situated at an elevation of over 4,000 feet. On that day, Johnson earned a promotion to brigadier general and the nickname "Old Allegheny."

In 1861, the Civil War was centered in western Virginia. As a result, reporters, writers, and sketch artist were sent to Grafton, Clarksburg, Philippi, Rich Mountain, and many other small towns and sites of action in the region. One of these men was David Hunter Strothers, who worked under the pen name Porte Crayon. The Berkeley Springs resident worked for the magazine *Harper's Weekly*. He later became colonel of the 3rd West Virginia Infantry.

Gen. William Rosecrans invented the Wheeling, or Rosecrans, ambulance. Early in the Civil War, there was no process for moving wounded soldiers. Even in small battles, there were hundreds of causalities. Ambulances and medical services developed rapidly to keep up with the growing number of causalities. The Wheeling Wagon and Carriage Company manufactured the Wheeling ambulance. Note the Partridge Photo Gallery at left, where many soldiers had their photographs taken. (Courtesy Diocese of Wheeling-Charleston Archives.)

The photography shop of Bennett Rider was located at Sycamore Dale near Clarksburg. Most towns had a photographer, who in many cases was the druggist. Many of Rider's photographs have survived. Photography had been around for 20 years, but the Civil War gave it a tremendous boost. The most common was the *carte de visite* (CDV), a two-inch-by-three-inch image mounted on card stock. The cost, less than 25¢ each, was affordable to every soldier. (Courtesy Harrison County Historical Society.)

This is an upstream view of Civil War–era Lowndes Mill in Clarksburg. The mill was located at the foot of Main Street on the West Fork River. It was in full production during the Civil War. The Army of Occupation and the Department of West Virginia were headquartered in Clarksburg at various times, and the town served as a major supply depot during the war. (Courtesy Harrison County Historical Society.)

This is the town of Grafton, with the railroad roundhouse in the foreground. Here, the Northwest Virginia Railroad, which ran to Parkersburg, made a junction with the Baltimore & Ohio Railroad, which traveled east to Baltimore and west to Wheeling. This was the headquarters of the Railroad District. Grafton was the most important junction on the railroad. At any time, a train with soldiers could be dispatched to any point on the line from here. (Courtesy the Baltimore & Ohio Railroad Museum.)

In this illustration from *Harper's Weekly*, Gen. Benjamin F. Kelley (seated, left) is seen with his staff. Kelley maintained a headquarters in Grafton. His staff included his son William (standing, left) and George Harrison (standing, second from right), an expert in working with and deploying the telegraph. The technology was critical during the war.

Gen. Robert E. Lee was a career Army officer who resigned to join the Confederacy. He was sent to western Virginia to coordinate Confederate efforts in the Trans-Allegheny region and assist Gen. William Loring. He was also charged with convincing Generals Henry Wise and John Floyd to work together. Lee, one of the great military strategists, was a failure in the mountains. But the lessons he learned propelled him to fame. On Sewell Mountain in Fayette County in September 1861, he was introduced to a fine horse that caught his eye. Lee would eventually purchase this horse, named Traveller. By this time, Lee had grown a beard and realized that he could not persuade Floyd and Wise to stop fighting each other. (Courtesy Rich Mountain Battlefield Foundation.)

Nathan Goff Jr. was in school at Georgetown when the war started. He went home to Clarksburg and joined a regiment that became the 3rd West Virginia Infantry. Goff was appointed adjutant of the regiment, then received a major's commission in the 4th West Virginia Cavalry. While escorting wagon trains, he came under attack. His horse was killed, and Goff was captured and sent to Libby Prison in Richmond. (Courtesy John Allen.)

This sketch of John Snider appeared in the *New York Illustrated News* on December 9, 1861. Snider served as a civilian scout for Gen. Benjamin F. Kelley. These scouts proved invaluable in the rugged mountains, as they knew the trails and the local citizens. There is very little documentation on the actions of these loyal men.

Three

1862
THE STRUGGLE

The beginning of 1862 saw a campaign by Stonewall Jackson to take Romney, but the weather and Union forces prove too much. The Union was repairing the railroad and fighting raiders. On March 30, 1862, the railroad returned to complete operation with the repair of the Harpers Ferry Bridge that Jackson had destroyed in June 1861. On that day, 3,800 cars moved across the bridge at Harpers Ferry. The next day, the first passenger train arrived in Wheeling from Baltimore, accompanied by a 100-gun salute.

In the Shenandoah Valley in late March, General Jackson began his famous Valley campaign. This caused the Union to pull soldiers from West Virginia to pursue Jackson. At times, Jackson tied up three armies by his fighting and maneuvering. In June, Jackson left the Valley to join Gen. Robert E. Lee at Richmond.

After its establishment, the Union Government of Virginia tried to gain acceptance by the citizens. The populace needed a working county government and to feel protected. The divided loyalties caused a breakdown of the civil government in Roane, Clay, Calhoun, and Wirt Counties. This resulted in the formation of guerrilla and militia groups for control of the area and protection of the people.

In an effort to win the hearts and minds of the citizens of the western Virginia counties, General Kelley planned an expedition to reestablish civil governments, assess guerrilla activities, and assure the citizens that the Restored Government of Virginia would protect them.

The work for statehood was continuing in Wheeling and Washington. The Restored Government of Virginia had to give approval for West Virginia statehood. Did it have the authority? This government had recruited and fielded over 20,000 soldiers and conducted government business, including wagging war. If it had the authority to do this, then it should have the full authority of a state under the constitution. If the secession of Virginia from the Union was considered constitutional, the secession of West Virginia from Virginia would also have to be accepted. John S. Carlile voted against the statehood bill. After that, Camp Carlile was renamed Camp Willey.

Clarksburg was a divided town, as was the rest of West Virginia. Before the Civil War, the militia was split along Union and secessionist lines. The two sides would drill on different days and, at the end of drills, would lock up the muskets, for everyone's safety. On May 23, 1861, the secessionists left town for Grafton and became part of the 31st Virginia Infantry. The Union boys mostly joined the 3rd West Virginia Infantry. The above photograph shows the Jackson home. This family was prominent Confederate sympathizers. The Union quartermaster was located in the stable near their home. The below photograph shows Waldamore, the home of Waldo Goff. He was the father of Nathan Goff Jr., the adjutant of the 3rd West Virginia Infantry and then major of the 4th West Virginia Cavalry. (Courtesy Harrison County Historical Society.)

Thomas Jackson, now and forever known as "Stonewall," started his Romney campaign on January 1, 1862. Jackson attacked the town of Bath, bombarded Hancock, and wrecked parts of the Chesapeake & Ohio Canal and the Baltimore & Ohio Railroad. He then moved on Romney, forcing Gen. Frederick Lander to evacuate the town.

This image depicts Frederick Lander evacuating Union forces from Romney on January 10, 1862. On January 5, he was en route to Romney to replace General Kelley, in Cumberland due to the wound he received at Philippi. Lander stopped in Hancock to defend it against Stonewall Jackson's attack. Jackson ended his bombardment when Kelley sent forces to attack Confederates at Blue's Gap, thus threatening Jackson's flank. It was at this point that Jackson then moved on Romney.

This is the memorial card for Frederick Lander. On February 14, 1862, Lander attacked a Confederate wagon train at Bloomery Gap, routing them but failing to capture the train. Lander blamed this on Col. Henry Anisansel of the 1st West Virginia Cavalry, who was then court-martialed. "The Great Natural American Soldier," Gen. Frederick Lander died at Paw Paw on March 2, 1862, from a wound received at Edwards Ferry.

John Hanson McNeill, known as Hanse, raised a company under the provisions of the Partisan Ranger Act, passed by the Confederate Congress on April 28, 1862. Many West Point officers considered the tactics used by partisans outside the bounds of legitimate warfare. McNeill's rangers conducted raids on the railroad and on Union wagon trains. On November 10, 1864, at Harrisonburg, Virginia, Captain McNeill died of wounds received at Mount Jackson.

The troops at Harpers Ferry were critical in the protection of the Baltimore & Ohio Railroad and the Chesapeake & Ohio Canal. On September 12, 1862, as part of Lee's Maryland campaign, Stonewall Jackson surrounded Harper Ferry. It was vital to the Confederate army that the town, along Lee's supply line, be forced to surrender. When Harpers Ferry fell, it was the largest surrender of Federal forces and equipment until the Battle of Corregidor in World War II.

Jesse Reno, born in Wheeling, was an 1846 graduate of West Point. He commanded the IX Corps at the Battle of South Mountain. On September 14, 1862, he was mortally wounded leading his troops at Fox's Gap. Reno saw his classmate Gen. Samuel Sturgis and said, "Hallo Sam, I am dead." The 39-year-old Reno died that evening and is buried in Oak Hill Cemetery in Georgetown.

This is a *Harper's Weekly* sketch of the Battle of Shepherdstown, sometimes known as the Battle of Boteler's Ford, or the Cement Mill. When Robert E. Lee retreated after the Battle of Antietam, Union forces crossed the Potomac River to pursue the Confederates. As the battle erupted, there was confusion, and most of the Union forces retreated. The Union troops that remained took a thrashing. Both sides occupied Shepherdstown during the Civil War. The majority of the town was pro-Confederate, with many of its men joining the 2nd Virginia Infantry. On the evening of September 18, 1862, General Lee's army moved from Maryland via Boteler's Ford, just below Shepherdstown. After the Battles of Antietam and Shepherdstown, the town became a hospital filled with the wounded.

Salt Sulphur Springs, built in 1820, was one of the many resort springs that existed in western Virginia. On August 20, 1862, Gen. Albert Gallatin Jenkins left the site with the 8th and 14th Virginia Cavalry on a raid against Federal forces. The first strike was on Buckhannon, where Jenkins captured the garrison and its arms and supplies. On September 4, he occupied Ravenswood, then he crossed into Ohio on September 12, completing a 500-mile raid. (Courtesy West Virginia State Archives.)

Maj. William Powell, of the 2nd West Virginia Cavalry, displayed great courage and leadership in his raid against Confederate forces at Sinking Creek Valley, Virginia, on November 26, 1862. With only 20 men, Powell charged and captured the enemy's camp, 500 strong, without the loss of man or gun. He became colonel of the regiment and was later promoted to general.

It was dangerous in the mountains; ambushes were frequent and hazard awaited any soldier that straggled. Guerrilla bands operated throughout western Virginia, including the Union Swamp Dragons and the Confederate Moccasin Rangers. There were many other bands in the mountains, some of who fought for a cause, some for personal gain, and others to settle old grudges. Some Union commanders had a policy of not taking guerrillas as prisoners.

Nancy Hart could not read or write, but she was fearless and deadly as a copperhead. While in her early 20s, she was a member of the Moccasin Rangers, a partisan group led by Perry Conley. Hart collected intelligence and delivered it to Confederates. She was taken prisoner, but she charmed her guard out of his musket and shot him dead. (Courtesy West Virginia State Archives.)

The second bridge at Gauley Bridge was built in February 1862 to replace the covered bridge burned by Confederates in July 1861. In August 1862, Gen. Jacob Cox removed over 7,000 troops to assist in the Maryland campaign, leaving Col. Joseph A.J. Lightburn with 5,000 men to defend the Kanawha Valley. Gen. William W. Loring moved against Lightburn's Union forces in September 1862. Lightburn ordered the bridge destroyed. (Courtesy West Virginia State Archives.)

This is an 1870s view of the city of Charleston. General Loring continued to push west in the Kanawha Valley, routing Union forces at Fayetteville. On September 13, 1862, Loring's forces attacked Lightburn's army at Charleston. After fighting all day, Lightburn retreated across the Elk River, cutting the bridge cables. General Loring then occupied the town. (Courtesy West Virginia State Archives.)

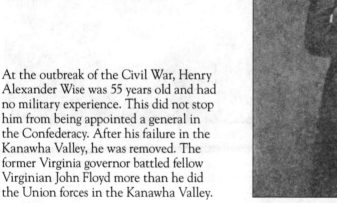

In September 1862, Gen. William W. Loring issued the proclamation shown here, in which he referred to the "counterfeit State Government." Pressure by Union troops forced Loring to abandon Charleston on October 8. Gen. John Echols held Charleston until October 29, but the threat from Union forces persuaded him to retreat from the Kanawha Valley. Union forces remained in control of the valley for the rest of the war.

At the outbreak of the Civil War, Henry Alexander Wise was 55 years old and had no military experience. This did not stop him from being appointed a general in the Confederacy. After his failure in the Kanawha Valley, he was removed. The former Virginia governor battled fellow Virginian John Floyd more than he did the Union forces in the Kanawha Valley.

Four

1863

STATEHOOD

The year 1863 started with President Lincoln issuing the Emancipation Proclamation, which freed all slaves in states in rebellion against the United States. The act only held force where Federal troops were in control of a part of a state. The Emancipation Proclamation did nothing for slaves in states that remained in the Union.

The West Virginia Constitution contained a provision for the emancipation of slaves. President Lincoln signed the West Virginia statehood bill on April 20, to take effect on June 20.

In April, in a coordinated raid, Gen. William Grumble Jones and John Imboden left the Shenandoah Valley with the mission of raiding the soon-to-be state of West Virginia. Their aim was to destroy railroads, steal horses and cattle, and recruit men into the Confederate army. In July 1861, General Lee had said, "The rupture of the railroad at Cheat River would be worth an army." Jones, however, failed to destroy the bridges there. The raid did capture 700 small arms and an artillery piece; destroyed 2 railroad trains, 16 railroad bridges, a tunnel, a large amount of oil-field equipment, and 150,000 barrels of oil; and seized 1,000 head of cattle and 1,200 horses.

The success of the Jones and Imboden raid forced changes on the military in West Virginia. The Department of West Virginia was formed, with Gen. Benjamin F. Kelley in command. Of the infantry regiments, three were mounted so they could purse horse-riding raiders. These mounted units were put under the command of a very capable cavalry officer, Gen. William W. Averell. Blockhouses would be constructed along the railroad.

Control of all the counties in West Virginia was moving forward. The Confederacy still had control of a few of the southern counties. General Averell's raids were putting pressure on the Confederates. Averell's target was the Virginia-Tennessee Railroad bridge across the New River. He was training the cavalry to get to the bridge, but the terrain was rugged. The biggest problem was carrying enough food for the men and horses.

The Tray Run Viaduct at Rowlesburg and the bridge crossing over the Cheat River were major objectives for Jones. His delay at Greenland Gap gave the Union defenders time to prepare for Jones. The 6th West Virginia Infantry put up a good fight, and Jones broke off the attack. Unknown to Jones, however, the Federals also retreated. The Tray Run Viaduct is depicted on the reverse side of the seal of West Virginia. (Courtesy the Baltimore & Ohio Railroad Museum.)

This covered bridge crossed the Cheat River on the Northwest Turnpike. After leaving Rowlesburg, General Jones's cavalry crossed here, moving toward Morgantown. Jones was in a very foul mood due to his failure to destroy the bridges at Rowlesburg. He gave orders to torch this bridge but spared it at the urging of the local citizens.

As Jones's Confederates roamed the countryside, moving toward Morgantown, they encountered three citizens, who took shots at the cavalrymen. The Confederates lined them up and shot them. One quick-thinking man played dead and escaped. This is one of the graves of the unfortunate men, in Oak Grove Cemetery.

The Morgantown suspension bridge over the Monongahela River is seen in this 1865 photograph by J.P. Shaffer. In April 1863, Gen. William "Grumble" Jones entered Morgantown, taking horses and cattle. One Confederate called Morgantown the "meanest Union hole we have been in yet." The rebels took all of the shoes, boots, and hats that could be found in the Morgantown stores. The Confederates rode south over the suspension bridge toward Fairmont without destroying it.

The Skinner Tavern was on the west side of Fairmont. When Jones's cavalry entered Fairmont, they found it defended. The Union troops put up a fight on the bridge that crossed the Monongahela River in front of Skinner Tavern. From this tavern, General Jones watched his veterans defeat the green Union soldiers. (Courtesy Richard "Dick" Duez.)

This bridge on the Monongahela River at Fairmont was built in 1852. The magnificent iron structure consisted of three spans totaling 615 feet. On April 29, 1863, the Confederates poured black powder into the structure's cast-iron tubular columns and ignited the explosive. After numerous tries at blowing up the bridge, the spans finally tumbled into the river. General Jones's Confederates then struck Bridgeport, destroying a train and burning bridges. (Courtesy the Baltimore & Ohio Railroad Museum.)

On April 30, Lt. Timothy F. Roane, 3rd West Virginia Cavalry, engaged General Jones's raiders at Maulby Bridge. He could only muster 65 men in his company, and an additional 20 citizens volunteered. Roane divided his command, leaving half to guard the ford, keeping Jones's main body from crossing the river. The other half fought the rearguard. The fight lasted about an hour.

Seen here is an oil derrick and tank of the period. On May 9, 1863, General Jones's men arrived at Burning Springs and destroyed an estimated 150,000 barrels of oil and equipment. Jones wrote, "By dark the oil from the tanks on the burning creek had reached the river, and the whole stream became a sheet of fire." This was the first time oil was destroyed for a military purpose.

The Northwest Academy's original use was as a school. During the war, it served as a barracks, military prison, and hospital. From 1861 to 1865, Clarksburg, situated on the Northwest Virginia Railroad, was the temporary home to hundreds of Union soldiers. After the Jones and Imboden raid, Clarksburg became the headquarters for the Department of West Virginia, commanded by Gen. Benjamin F. Kelley.

Gen. Thomas J. "Stonewall" Jackson proved himself one of the greatest tactical generals of all time. From his celebrated Shenandoah Valley campaign, which is still studied by the military, to his flank march and attack at Chancellorsville, he showed his leadership abilities. On May 2, 1863, Jackson was accidently shot, and his wounded arm was amputated. On May 10, at Guinea Station, he died of pneumonia.

Lindsey Institute in Wheeling became West Virginia's first capitol. The institute was chartered in 1814, and this building was completed in 1858. The building served as the capitol from June 20, 1863, to April 1, 1870. (Courtesy Diocese of Wheeling-Charleston Archives.)

Arthur I. Boreman, a resident of Tyler County, was a lawyer, a member of the Virginia Assembly, and he presided over the Second Wheeling Convention. Elected as the first governor of West Virginia, he took office on June 20, 1863. Boreman had his hands full with the war, as the Confederates still controlled some of West Virginia's southern counties and the outcome of the war was still in question.

Wheeling was a well-fortified town, as is apparent here at the bridge over Wheeling Creek. There were two independent companies in the city as well as troops guarding prisoners, waiting for transportation, or waiting to muster into a regiment. The Wheeling government was a target of the Confederates, but the only fire that Wheeling received during the war was verbal, from the secessionists.

On June 20, 1863, West Virginia became the 35th state of the Union. The celebration in Wheeling included the ringing of bells, firing of cannons, and speeches. The US Custom House (seen here) had been the site of a tremendous amount of action since the first Wheeling Convention. It was the capitol of the Restored Government of Virginia, and it gave birth to West Virginia.

Waitman T. Willey, a lawyer from Morgantown, was elected US senator for the Restored Government of Virginia. When John Carlile tried to defeat West Virginia statehood, Willey worked to sell it to the senate. He authored the Willey Amendment to the West Virginia statehood bill, which called for the gradual emancipation of slavery in the state. He was elected a US senator for West Virginia.

John Snyder Carlile was a delegate from Harrison County who resided in Clarksburg. He served as a state senator, a delegate to the Virginia Constitutional Convention of 1850–1851, and a congressman. He voted against secession in 1861 and headed the movement to break away from Virginia. He was elected to the US Senate for the Restored Government of Virginia. Carlile, who had drafted the statehood bill for West Virginia, later changed his mind regarding the issue. He sought to sabotage statehood efforts and voted against the bill.

An important crossing point on the Potomac River, Watkins Ferry was located directly across the river from Williamsport, Maryland. This main house, known as Maidstone-on-the-Potomac, was built in 1741. The ferry was used by George Washington and Edward Braddock. Thousands of men crossed on the ferry after the Battle of Gettysburg. (Courtesy Berkeley County Historical Society.)

Confederate general James Johnston Pettigrew led a division at Gettysburg. His troops took part in Pickett's Charge (the name should have been Pickett-Pettigrew-Trimble's Charge). During the retreat from Gettysburg, Pettigrew was mortally wounded at Falling Waters. He was taken across the Potomac to Edgewood Manor plantation. On July 17, 1863, General Pettigrew died. (Courtesy Berkeley County Historical Society.)

The hoppers in Organ Cave are relics of Confederate saltpeter operations. Soldiers were detailed to operate the mine here beginning in 1861, ultimately producing a large percentage of the saltpeter used in the production of the Confederate army's gunpowder. The saltpeter was shipped to Southern factories. On August 19, 1863, Gen. William W. Averell led a cavalry expedition to destroy this operation.

This Bulltown covered bridge was on the Weston and Gauley Bridge Turnpike, where it crosses the Little Kanawha River. The turnpike connects the Staunton and Parkersburg Turnpike with the Kanawha Valley. Bulltown was garrisoned by Union troops during most of the war. On October 13, 1863, Confederate general William L. Jackson attacked Bulltown. After 12 hours of fighting, Jackson broke off the attack.

Bart Clark, of the 3rd West Virginia Mounted Infantry, was wounded at the battle of White Sulphur Springs. Gen. William W. Averell went to Lewisburg to seize the Virginia State Law Library for the new state and to destroy the Virginia-Tennessee Railroad. Col. George Patton commanded the Confederate forces. The battle started on August 26, 1863, and lasted until the next day. Due to lack of progress and ammunition, Averell retreated to Beverly.

STATE OF WEST VIRGINIA,

_____TOWNSHIP OF _____COUNTY, } TO-WIT :

I,_____do solemnly swear that I have not, since the first day of June, eighteen hundred and sixty-one, voluntarily borne arms against the United States, the reorganized government of Virginia or the State of West Virginia ; that I have not voluntarily given aid, comfort or assistance to persons engaged in armed hostility against the United States, the reorganized government of Virginia or the State of West Virginia ; that I have not sought, accepted, exercised or attempted to exercise, any office or appointment whatever, under any authority or pretended authority hostile or inimical to the United States, the reorganized government of Virginia or the State of West Virginia ; that I will support the constitution of the United States and the constitution of this State ; and that I take this oath freely, without any mental reservation or purpose of evasion.

_____

Subscribed and sworn to before me this_____day of_____186__

_____

Registrar_____ _____ _____township.

Any citizen could be required to sign a loyalty oath. If a suspicious person was captured, an oath could be issued by an officer at that time. If a person refused or was charged with a crime against the Union, they could be sent to a prison in Wheeling or to Camp Chase, Ohio. Note that the oath specifies the reorganized government of Virginia.

This panoramic photograph of Clarksburg was taken in 1862 by Bennett Rider. Clarksburg was occupied by Federal troops for the entire war. In July 1863, the headquarters for the Department of West Virginia was established here. Because of Confederate raids on the railroad in the eastern panhandle, the department headquarters was moved to Cumberland. (Courtesy Harrison County Historical Society.)

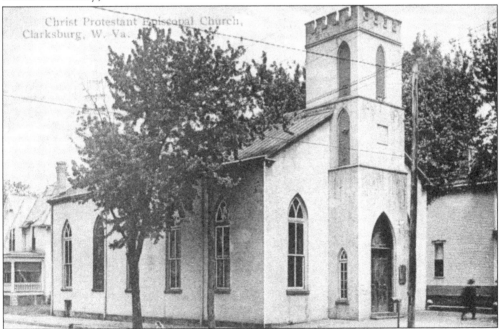

The Presbyterian Church of Clarksburg was used to quarter soldiers during the Civil War. Although many tents and huts were erected to quarter the men, soldiers occupied every public building at one time or another. It was good for the economy but could be hard on the town. Besides the school, every church in town sheltered sick soldiers, some of whom did a great deal of damage to the buildings.

Gen. William W. Averell (left) led a raid from Beverly to destroy the Virginia-Tennessee Railroad. Averell, a West Point graduate, was a superior cavalry officer. He moved his command south and discovered that the Confederates were entrenched on Droop Mountain. The Confederates were command by John Echols (below). Echols had his men prepare fighting positions on the 3,000-foot mountain. On November 6, 1863, Averell sent three regiments up the front of the mountain and then sent two regiments to flank the Confederates. The Union was successful in overrunning the Confederates. Averell was too burdened with prisoners and captured supplies to move on the railroad.

Five

1864
TOTAL WAR

In 1864, the war moved almost entirely out of West Virginia, except in the eastern panhandle. President Lincoln found a general, Ulysses S. Grant, who would fight and destroy the enemy. Grant tried to coordinate simultaneous attacks against the Confederacy. Sometimes, that was easier said than done. Not all of the generals could wage war the way Grant wanted them to. He eventually got the correct generals in place, but it took time. Grant knew that, to end the war, he had to destroy General Lee's army.

Pres. Abraham Lincoln was in the midst of a reelection campaign in 1864. His opponent was his former general, George B. McClellan. The citizens of the North were war weary. They wanted an end to the conflict. The soldiers still loved McClellan, but they did not vote for him. Lincoln's goal was to win the war, but politics sometimes got in the way. Union victories in the fall of 1864 ensured Lincoln's reelection.

By the summer, most West Virginia soldiers had moved out of the state to the Shenandoah Valley. By the end of the year, their new home was in the trenches around Petersburg. The Army of West Virginia under Gen. George Crook had success against the Virginia-Tennessee Railroad and in the Shenandoah Valley. The war got hard for these soldiers. The marches got long, and the fighting became ferocious. In 1864, the conflict became total war. Union general Phil Sheridan burned all crops and barns in the Shenandoah Valley. Confederate general John McCausland tried to collect ransoms from towns, threatening to burn them if he was not paid. McCausland burned Chambersburg, Pennsylvania. The soldiers were constantly on the move, either marching or fighting. Many of West Virginia's finest men sacrificed their lives for the Union and the Lost Cause.

The German general Franz Sigel replaced Brigadier General Kelley as commander of the Department of West Virginia on March 12, 1864. The reason for the change was that President Lincoln needed the German vote, and Sigel was a major general. Sigel moved his army from Martinsburg, up the Shenandoah Valley, and was badly defeated by Confederates at New Market. Of Sigel, it was said that he "was not just incompetent; he was a fool."

Maj. Gen. David Hunter replaced Sigel on May 21, 1864, and launched an attack into the Shenandoah Valley. He burned down the Virginia Military Academy but was defeated by Gen. Jubal Early at Lynchburg. After a hard retreat over the mountains and into the Kanawha Valley, Hunter's army took steamboats on the Kanawha River, up the Ohio River, to board trains at Parkersburg. They arrived at Martinsburg to meet Early's advance on Washington.

The Union post at New Creek started as a winter camp. Log cabins were constructed to quarter the soldiers. The man in the foreground leaning against the cabin is Col. James A. Mulligan. In November 1864, Confederate Thomas Rosser captured the town in a surprise attack. The capture included supplies, ammunition, and most of the Union soldiers. Several miles of railroad track was destroyed before Union forces routed the foe.

Daniel Frost, a Ravenswood newspaper publisher, was Speaker of the House for the Restored Government of Virginia. Becoming colonel of the 11th West Virginia Infantry, he was wounded at the Battle of Cool Springs on July 18, 1864. Frost requested to see a relative, who lived on the battlefield. Eben Frost declined, replying, "If he had stayed home, he would not have been shot." Colonel Frost died of his wounds.

New Creek was an important supply depot along the Potomac River and the Baltimore & Ohio Railroad. It was from here that many military operations began. In October 1861, General Kelley departed New Creek to fight the Battle of Romney. General Averell launched his mounted raid from here in December 1863. Forts Piano and Kelley were constructed here to protect the railroad.

CAMP ﾟ 1ˢᵗ Vᴀ Vol Infᵗʸ. North Mountain Vᴀ. Jᴀɴ' 26ᵗʰ 1863.

The North Mountain station was on the Baltimore & Ohio Railroad in Berkeley County. This site was garrisoned during the Civil War to protect the railroad. The 1st West Virginia Infantry was stationed here in January 1863. The regimental sergeant major, Lucian Gray, was a very good artist. He drew this image of the regiment and had it made into a *cartes de visite* (CDV).

On March 24, 1864, James Giles, a Marshall County native, enlisted in the 7th West Virginia Infantry. Standing five feet, four inches tall, with blue eyes, light hair, and a fair complexion, he looked younger than his 18 years. The 7th was quartered in the earthen Fort Davis at the siege of Petersburg. On October 27, 1864, at the battle of Hatcher Run, Giles was killed, leaving behind desolate parents.

Benjamin Field was a farmer from Preston County who joined the 3rd West Virginia Infantry. This mounted unit became the 6th West Virginia Cavalry. Field enlisted in Newberg on June 28, 1861. He died on July 17, 1864 at General Hospital in Cumberland, Maryland, of tetanus. Field had suffered a contused wound from falling from a horse on June 15. He is buried at the Antietam National Cemetery.

Col. James A. Mulligan, commander of the 23rd Illinois Infantry, was in West Virginia for much of the war. He was one of the few Union commanders to launch offensive action during the Jones and Imboden raid. Mulligan's men built Fort Mulligan in Petersburg. He was commanding a brigade at Second Kernstown when he was mortally wounded. He died on June 24, 1864.

Union colonel James Mulligan supervised the construction of Fort Mulligan between August and December 1863. These works, in Petersburg, protected the South Branch Valley and its Unionist residents, and it served as an auxiliary depot for Federal military supplies. Col. Joseph Thoburn ordered the evacuation of Fort Mulligan on January 31, 1864, when Confederate general Jubal A. Early's army threatened an attack.

Gen. Albert Gallatin Jenkins, from Cabell County, was a Confederate cavalry commander. He operated independently in the early years of the war. In 1862, he carried the Confederate flag into Ohio for the first time. Jenkins commanded Confederate forces at the battle of Cloyd's Mountain, where he was wounded and captured. His arm required amputation at the shoulder. Jenkins did not survive the operation and died on May 21, 1864.

Joseph Thoburn was the surgeon for the three-month regiment and was commissioned colonel of the 1st West Virginia Infantry. During Sheridan's 1864 Valley campaign, Thoburn commanded a division in the Army of West Virginia. On the early morning of October 19, 1864, General Early's Confederates attacked Thoburn's division, sending them reeling north. Thoburn was mortally wounded while trying to rally his men. He is buried in Wheeling.

Seymour Beach Conger, a major in the 3rd West Virginia Cavalry, was leading his regiment at the Battle of Moorefield on August 6, 1864, when he was killed. This battle was the result of Gen. William Averill's dogged pursuit of Gen. John McCasuland after the burning of Chambersburg. Averill said of Conger, "Brave, steadfast and modest, when he fell this command lost one of its best soldiers."

John McCausland, a graduate of the Virginia Military Institute, was a professor of mathematics until the Civil War. After General Jenkins was killed, McCausland assumed command. McCausland took his brigade to Chambersburg and burned it down when the townspeople could not pay the ransom. At Appomattox, McCausland escaped with his cavalry. (Courtesy West Virginia Archives.)

New Creek, present-day Keyser, maintained a large cavalry camp throughout the war. This photograph shows the camp of the 22nd Pennsylvania Cavalry, originally known as the Ringgold Cavalry. In the summer of 1861, the unit consisted of one company. The cavalry crossed the Mason-Dixon Line and offered its services to the Union government of Virginia. The Ringgolds became known for their fighting ability and was General Kelley's favorite unit.

This is the commissary at Sir John's Run in Morgan County. This site was garrisoned for most of the war to protect the railroad trestle, located where Sir John's Run flows into the Potomac River. The 20th Pennsylvania Cavalry is seen here, but the 15th West Virginia Infantry was stationed here for most of 1863.

Jefferson Spencer Brent, born in 1833, was the slave of William Johnson of Bridgeport. Brent ran off and joined the 5th Massachusetts Cavalry. On July 4, 1864, he wrote to his wife from Point Lookout, where the regiment was guarding prisoners. Brent expressed happiness with his regiment. In 1860, the slave population in the counties that became West Virginia was 18,371. Harrison County had 582 slaves. (Courtesy Richard Duez.)

The 1864 presidential election proved that the republic could function during wartime. George B. McClellan, the former general, ran against President Lincoln. At the start of 1864, the reelection of Lincoln was not a sure thing. However, the war started going in the Union's favor, and major victories by Generals Grant, Sherman, and Sheridan sealed Lincoln's win. West Virginia voted overwhelmingly for Lincoln (23,152) over McClellan (10,438).

Six

1865

THE UNION IS PRESERVED

As the last year of the war began, it was apparent that it was a matter of time before the Confederacy capitulated. The year found many of the West Virginia units in and around Petersburg, Virginia, participating in Gen. Ulysses S. Grant's siege of Gen. Robert E. Lee's Army of Northern Virginia.

The 1st, 2nd, and 3rd West Virginia Cavalries were active in chasing down the retreating Confederate army in March and April 1865. In these two months, 15 Medals of Honor were awarded to troopers in the cavalry units.

Shesh B. Howe, a captain in the 1st West Virginia Cavalry, was killed leading his regiment in a charge on April 8, 1865, at Appomattox Courthouse. He was killed at the close of that obstinate engagement, at the hour of midnight. For this gallant action, Howe was posthumously promoted to major.

As the guns fell silent at Appomattox, West Virginia regiments witnessed the sobering event. On the field were three cavalry regiments (1st, 2nd, and 3rd) and five infantry regiments (7th, 10th, 11th, 12th, and 15th). There were West Virginians on the Confederate side at Appomattox as well, including the 2nd Virginia Infantry, the 31st Virginia Infantry, and the 8th Virginia Cavalry. The 31st Virginia had been at Philippi to witness the first shots fired.

Soon after the surrender of the Army of Northern Virginia, and as Abraham Lincoln set out to reconcile the nation's former antagonists, an assassin's bullet ended the president's life. One of the men that hunted down John Wilkes Booth was Col. Everton Conger. He had received serious wounds as captain in the 3rd West Virginia Cavalry. Conger, the brother of Maj. Seymour B. Conger, received the largest portion of the reward for the capture of Booth.

The West Virginia regiments were quickly mustered out of service. The 1st, 2nd, and 3rd Cavalries led off the Grand Review in Washington. One regiment, the 6th Veteran West Virginia Cavalry, was sent out west to Fort Leavenworth, Kansas, for a year to fight Indians and to guard stagecoaches.

The Hampshire County Poorhouse was where the McNeill's Rangers met on February 20, 1865. Jessie McNeill and 60 men mounted reliable horses. The Confederates, wearing Union overcoats as they made their way through the snow to Cumberland, tricked their way past the pickets. In Cumberland, they convinced other soldiers that they were a cavalry company from New Creek. Gen. George Crook was staying at the hotel and train station in Cumberland. Adjacent to these buildings was the Revere Hotel, where General Kelley was quartered. McNeill's Rangers captured the two generals and started riding down Baltimore Street to the Chesapeake & Ohio Canal towpath to Wiley's Ford, then crossed the Potomac River. The hard riding paid off, as McNeill delivered the generals to Richmond. (Courtesy Fort Mill Ridge Foundation.)

Seven

1867–2013

VETERANS, REUNIONS, AND MEMORIALS

When the war ended, many issues faced the returning veterans. The situation was more difficult for the Confederates, who had left their Virginia home and returned to what was now West Virginia. At first, many of the soldiers sought to forget the war and get on with their lives. It was time to get a job and raise a family. However, forgetting the greatest adventure of their lives would not easily happen. After a few years, the Grand Army of the Republic (GAR), an organization for Union veterans, and the United Confederate Veterans (UCV), an organization for Confederate veterans, were formed and began holding annual events.

West Virginia issued medals to all of the Union soldiers who served honorably in a West Virginia unit. The medals were prized possessions for these veterans. The first monument to the war was a Confederate Monument in Romney in 1867. No Union monument appeared until 1880, in Wheeling. In a poor state like West Virginia, spending money on monuments was not a high priority. Parkersburg has a cannon that was dedicated to the Union soldiers, but the Parkersburg Confederates erected a statue of a Confederate. While some may look at the cannon and ask about its significance, the statue tells the story.

Starting in the 1880s and until the 1920s, there were many reunions in the state. Clarksburg held a Blue and Gray Reunion in 1887. This is unusual, as most reunions were for one side or the other. In other states, such joint reunions came later. They may have started earlier in West Virginia because it was such a divided state during the war.

In the later years, veterans, now gray, made trips to visit the old battlefields where they fought in their youth. In 1928, after many of the veterans were gone, West Virginia created Droop Mountain Battlefield Park.

It is important to remember the sacrifices these soldiers made. The current generation is charged with maintaining the monuments, preserving the battlefields, and decorating the soldiers' graves. The men and women of 1861 are owed a great deal. The results of that war changed things forever. A people become free, a state was born, the republic was saved, and America started its journey to become the world's leader.

Confederate Monument in City Park, Parkersburg, W. Va.

The Confederate Monument at Parkersburg is in the city park. The Parkersburg Chapter of the United Daughters of the Confederacy dedicated this monument in 1908 to Confederate dead. During the Civil War, Parkersburg was a very strong Union town.

The Confederate Monument in Union is located at the edge of town. On August 29, 1901, a monument to the *Confederate Soldiers from Monroe County* was dedicated. The total height of the monument is 19 feet, 6 inches, and its weight is about 40,000 pounds. The cornerstone of the monument was laid on September 6, 1900, with Masonic ceremonies, and in it were deposited the rolls of the companies of Confederate troops organized in Monroe County.

Confederate Monument in Union, West Virginia

This Confederate Monument in the Indian Mound Cemetery in Romney was erected on September 26, 1867, making it the first Confederate monument. The Confederate Memorial Association was formed in June 1866. The total cost of the monument was $1,174.54. Inscribed on the front is the following: "The Daughters of Old Hampshire erect this tribute of affection to her heroic Sons, who fell in defense of Southern Rights."

The Confederate Monument in Lewisburg was unveiled on June 14, 1906. The base is composed of four feet of native limestone and nine feet of granite, topped with a six-foot, seven-inch bronze sculpture. W.L. Sheppard of Richmond, Virginia, designed the monument.

The statue of Thomas J. Jackson was unveiled by the Daughters of the Confederacy on May 10, 1953, on the Clarksburg Courthouse plaza. The statue of General Jackson and his horse, Little Sorrel, was created by New York sculptor Charles Keck. This was a duplicate of his statue in Charlottesville, Virginia, that was dedicated in 1921. A rededication of the monument was held on May 10, 2013. Thomas J. Jackson was born on Clarksburg on January 21, 1824. On May 2, 1863, he was wounded at Chancellorsville. His arm was amputated. On May 10, 1863, Jackson died at Guinea Station. (Courtesy Lemeul Muniz.)

The Union Soldiers and Sailors Memorial Commission erected the Union Monument in Charleston in 1930. It is dedicated to the Union soldiers from West Virginia who served in the Civil War. A plaque on the north side of the monument is inscribed with Lincoln's Gettysburg Address. It is located on Kanawha Boulevard near the capitol.

This Union Monument in Huntington, at the corner of Fifth Avenue and Ninth Street, is no longer there. It was dedicated by the Huntington Bailey Post of the Grand Army of the Republic sometime around 1895 to honor the Union veterans of the Civil War from Cabell County. The story goes that it was being moved to Ritter Park on August 6, 1915, but was instead taken to the dump.

This monument on Valley Mountain, at the campsite of Robert E. Lee and his troops, was erected in 1909. It is dedicated to the dead of the 21st and 48th Virginia Infantry regiments. Disease paid a heavy toll in that very rainy summer of 1861. (Courtesy Hunter Lesser.)

This Union Monument is in Woodlawn Cemetery. The Ladies of the Meade Circle of the Grand Army of the Republic erected the monument, which was dedicated on May 30, 1930. Near this monument are the graves of Gov. Francis Pierpont and his wife, Julia. At least 100 Civil War soldiers are buried in Woodlawn Cemetery.

This Confederate Monument was unveiled at Mingo in Randolph County on July 23, 1913. The three veterans are, from left to right, George Washington Painter, 19th Virginia Infantry; William H. Brady, 26th Virginia Infantry; and John Stewart, 22nd Virginia Infantry. The monument was the work of Camp Pegram, United Confederate Veterans. It is dedicated "To the memory of the Confederate soldiers of Randolph County and vicinity." This includes all soldiers who died on Valley Mountain in 1861 while General Lee was encamped here. The ceremony was attended by 1,000 people. (Courtesy Don Rice.)

The Union Monument in Ripley, Jackson County, was dedicated on June 23, 1915. It was a well-attended event. Officers from the Shotto GAR Post and officers of the Department of West Virginia GAR hosted the event. Former governor George W. Atkinson was the speaker. The monument, on the courthouse square, is flanked by two mountain howitzers. (Courtesy Mike Chancey.)

W. VA. MOUNTAINEER STATUE, STATE CAPITOL GROUNDS,
CHARLESTON, W. VA.

The Grand Army of the Republic and the Women's Relief Society erected the West Virginia
Militia Monument. The monument was dedicated in 1912 to honor the men who, on April 15,
1861, answered the Union call and to the hallowed memories of the brave men and devoted women
who saved West Virginia to the Union. It is located on the northeast side of the capitol.

The 7th West Virginia Monument was dedicated at Gettysburg on East Cemetery Hill on November 28, 1896. On the evening of July 2, 1863, the 7th West Virginia Infantry, with Carroll's Brigade, was ordered to move to the top of the hill. There, they found the Confederates overrunning the artillery battery. The Union forces charged the enemy, driving them off the hill.

The Union Monument at Kingwood in Preston County was dedicated by the Kelley Post of the GAR. Work on the monument started in 1895, and it was dedicated in 1903. A cannon that had been at Fort Sumner was added to the monument. The Kelley Post is named for Gen. Benjamin Franklin Kelley.

The Union Monument in Morgantown is in the Oak Grove Cemetery, where many Civil War veterans are buried. Unveiled in 1905, the monument was built by J.E. Watts & Company of Morgantown. There is also a brass cannon in front of the monument.

The Confederate Monument in the Spring Hill Cemetery in Huntington was unveiled on June 3, 1900. Hundreds of Confederate veterans from the surrounding counties participated in the procession from the Cabell County Courthouse to the cemetery. "Taps" was sounded by 8th Virginia Cavalry veteran Sylvester Summers on an old battered bugle that he had carried during the war. This monument had a soldier on top, but it blew down during a 1970 storm. Camp Garnet of the Sons of Confederate Veterans dedicated the monument.

The monument *Abraham Lincoln Walks at Midnight* stands in front of the West Virginia state capitol. It was dedicated on June 20, 1974. In 1933, Fred M. Torrey sculpted a three-and-a-half-foot model of this statue. Thirty years later, on February 12, 1970 (Lincoln's birthday), it was brought to Charleston, and four years later, the full-size statue was dedicated.

The Wheeling Union Monument, dedicated "To the defenders of the Union. 1861–1865," was erected by the Soldiers Aid Society of Wheeling in 1880. This is the first Union monument erected in West Virginia, which is appropriate, since the first military unit was formed in Wheeling. The monument was originally located in downtown Wheeling, but it was moved to Wheeling Park.

The Reno Monument at Fox's Gap in South Mountain, Maryland, was dedicated on September 14, 1889. Jesse Reno, born in Wheeling, was killed here on September 14, 1862. The survivors of Gen. Jesse L. Reno's IX Corps came back to South Mountain to unveil the monument 27 years after Reno's death. In 1989, at its 100th anniversary, the monument was rededicated.

This Union Monument in Rymer Cemetery was dedicated in 1908 by the Grand Army of the Republic, Gooch Post No. 88. This cemetery is near Mannington, on Buffalo Road. The post was named for Charles L. Gooch of the 14th West Virginia Infantry, who was killed on July 20, 1864, at Carter's Farm near Winchester, Virginia.

His comrades dedicated this monument, located in Jollytown, Pennsylvania, to Jesse Taylor. He was the first soldier from Green County, Pennsylvania, and the 7th West Virginia Infantry to be killed. At the Battle of Romney on October 26, 1861, Taylor was shot and killed. The monument is flanked by an 1861 Parrott gun and two Coehorn mortars.

The Thomas J. Stonewall Jackson Monument in Charleston was dedicated on September 27, 1910. It present site is in front of the state capitol complex. The statue was commissioned and erected by the Charleston Chapter No. 151, United Daughters of the Confederacy. The sculptor, Moses Jacob Ezekiel, was a Virginia Military Institute graduate who served at the Battle of New Market on May 15, 1864.

Battery C First West Virginia Light Artillery Monument was dedicated at Gettysburg in the National Cemetery on November 28, 1896. Capt. Wallace Hill commanded the battery. On July 3, 1863, the battery's Parrott guns were engaged during Pickett's Charge, expending 1,120 rounds of ammunition. During the Gettysburg's battle, the battery had two men killed, two wounded, and five horses killed. The battery's original nickname was "Pierpont's," but it became known as Hill's Battery. During the spring of 1864, the battery moved to the defenses of Washington at Fort Ward.

ERECTED BY THE STATE OF
WEST VIRGINIA
TO COMMEMORATE THE
VALOR AND FIDELITY
OF THE
FIRST WEST VIRGINIA CAVALRY

The 1st West Virginia Cavalry Monument was dedicated at Gettysburg, on the Taneytown Road, on November 28, 1896. Col. Nathaniel Richmond commanded the regiment. The 1st was in Elon Farnsworth's brigade of Judson Kilpatrick's division. The action in the Gettysburg campaign started on June 30 at Hanover. There was a charge on July 3, and a wagon train was captured on July 4 while pursuing Lee's retreating army.

On June 20, 2013, West Virginia's 150th birthday, Pendleton County dedicated a monument of a Civil War soldier that represents both the Union and the Confederacy. It was a joint effort by the Brigadier General James Boggs Camp No. 1706, Sons of Confederate Veterans, and the Sons of Union Veterans of the Civil War. James Boggs was a Confederate soldier, and his brother John Boggs was a Union soldier from Pendleton County.

This Confederate Monument on Droop Mountain is outside the park's boundaries on private land. There is no apparent explanation as to why it is located there, except that this is where the Confederate artillery was located. The Captain E.D. Camden Chapter of the Daughters of the Confederacy of Sutton dedicated the monument on July 4, 1831.

There are two Union Monuments at Droop Mountain. The photograph at right shows the monument to 1st Sgt. John D. Baxter, Company F, 10th West Virginia Infantry. On November 6, 1863, while leading a charge on the enemy's position, he was mortally wounded. He is buried in the Grafton National Cemetery. In the photograph below is the monument to Lt. Henry Bender, Company F, 10th West Virginia Infantry. He was in command of the company as it made the final assault that broke the Confederate line. Droop Mountain became the first state park in West Virginia, in 1928. Droop Mountain was not the largest battle in West Virginia, but it is remembered because most of the men that fought there were West Virginians.

In the Moorefield Cemetery, Mount Olivet, the Confederate Monument was erected in 1873. The monument's east face reads: "Erected in 1873 by the Memorial Association of Hardy County to the memory of our Confederate dead, who fell in the late war, in defense of Constitutional Liberty and our homes, 14 unknown." Many Confederate soldiers are buried around the monument. This includes "Hanse" McNeill.

The Union Monument for the soldiers of Marshall County in Moundsville was dedicated on May 19, 1909. At the dedication, over 250 Civil War veterans attended. On either side of the monument stand two brass cannons. One of the cannons was captured at Droop Mountain, and the other saw service in the Mexican-American and Civil Wars.

The monument to Gordon Battelle was dedicated on July 6, 1913, in Newport Cemetery in Newport, Ohio. A likeness of Battelle is on top the monument. He was a clergyman and educator. In October 1861, he was elected as a delegate to the Restored Government of Virginia Constitutional Convention. He volunteered to be the chaplain for the 1st West Virginia Infantry. Battelle died of typhoid fever on August 7, 1862.

The Union Monument for the soldiers of Hancock County was dedicated on May 30, 1886, by the W.A. Atkinson GAR Post, No. 18. The monument sits at the county courthouse in New Cumberland. On the monument is a list of the soldiers from Hancock County.

The Confederate Monument in Hinton was dedicated in 1914. It is a 15-foot statue of a Confederate soldier. One panel pays tribute to the Southern women: "Sacred to the memory of the noble women of the Confederacy, who suffered more and lost as much with less glory, than the Confederate soldier."

This is one of 25 Civil War markers erected in 1910 throughout Jefferson County. The Henry Kyd Douglas Camp of the Sons of Confederate Veterans identified Civil War actions in Jefferson County and placed numbered markers at the sites. A booklet, *Military Operations in Jefferson County*, was produced that describes the action at each marker.

The John Brown Monument is on the approximate spot where the engine house originally stood but about 60 feet higher in elevation. A railroad embankment is on the original site. In the 1880s, a committee formed by Frederick Douglass raised money for a granite marker for the site of the engine house. This monument was dedicated in 1898.

IN MEMORY OF
PVT LUKE QUINN
ONLY MARINE KILLED IN JOHN BROWN'S RAID — OCTOBER 18, 1859
PVT LUKE QUINN CAME FROM IRELAND IN 1535, AND ENLISTED IN THE
MARINE CORPS IN 1855 IN BROOKLYN, NY. HE WAS SENT TO SEA DUTY,
THEN TRANSFERRED TO MARINE BARRACKS IN WASHINGTON, DC.
HE CAME TO HARPERS FERRY WITH LIEUT. COLONEL ROBERT E. LEE. THEN
WAS KILLED IN THE STORMING OF THE ENGINE HOUSE. HIS FUNERAL
WAS IN ST. PETERS CATHOLIC CHURCH BY FATHER MICHAEL COSTELLO,
AND HE WAS BURIED IN ST. PETERS CATHOLIC CEMETERY.

The Luke Quinn Monument was the idea of a group of Harpers Ferry/Bolivar District veterans.
In May 2011, the monument was erected. The monument is on Potomac Street in Harpers Ferry,
near the original position of the engine house. It honors Marine private Luke Quinn, killed
assaulting the engine house during John Brown's raid.

Allen Bonner stands beside this Confederate Monument on Mount Iser in Beverly, erected in 1908 by the Randolph Chapter of the Daughters of the Confederacy. This marks the mass grave of 69 soldiers and 1 civilian who were killed at the Battle of Rich Mountain, near Beverly. The civilian casualty was John Hughes, a local politician mistakenly killed by Confederate soldiers during the battle. The monument was dedicated on September 30, 1908: "To The Confederate Soldiers Resting Here And To All Who Wore The Gray Lest We Forget." (Courtesy Randolph County Historical Society.)

This monument, located at Elkwater, Randolph County, honors Lt. Col. Augustine Washington, the great-grandnephew of Gen. George Washington and the last Washington to own Mount Vernon. Washington was Gen. Robert E. Lee's aide-de-camp. While reconnoitering, he was killed by Federal pickets. Lee's son Rooney was accompanying Washington. When Lee's horse was killed, he escaped on Washington's horse.

ON THE NIGHT OF OCTOBER 16, 1859. HEYWARD SHEPHERD, AN INDUSTRIOUS AND RESPECTED COLORED FREEMAN, WAS MORTALLY WOUNDED BY JOHN BROWN'S RAIDERS. IN PURSUANCE OF HIS DUTIES AS AN EMPLOYEE OF THE BALTIMORE AND OHIO RAILROAD COMPANY, HE BECAME THE FIRST VICTIM OF THIS ATTEMPTED INSURRECTION.

THIS BOULDER IS ERECTED BY THE UNITED DAUGHTERS OF THE CONFEDERACY AND THE SONS OF CONFEDERATE VETERANS AS A MEMORIAL TO HEYWARD SHEPHERD, EXEMPLIFYING THE CHARACTER AND FAITHFULNESS OF THOUSANDS OF NEGROES WHO, UNDER MANY TEMPTATIONS THROUGHOUT SUBSEQUENT YEARS OF WAR, SO CONDUCTED THEMSELVES THAT NO STAIN WAS LEFT UPON A RECORD WHICH IS THE PECULIAR HERITAGE OF THE AMERICAN PEOPLE, AND AN EVERLASTING TRIBUTE TO THE BEST IN BOTH RACES

The Heyward Shepherd Monument in Harpers Ferry was dedicated on October 10, 1931. Shepherd was the first death in John Brown's raid. Shepherd, a free black man, was a porter for the B&O Railroad when Brown's men killed him on the morning of October 17, 1859. This controversial monument suggests that Shepherd resisted Brown's war on slavery. It is also a veiled attempt to suggest that the slaves support the Confederacy.

The 3rd West Virginia Cavalry Monument was dedicated at Gettysburg, on Buford Avenue, on November 28, 1896. Companies A and C of the 3rd Cavalry were command by Capt. Seymour B. Conger. The companies were in Col. Thomas Devin's brigade, in John Buford's division. The companies saw action on McPherson's Ridge on July 1, 1863. It was the first fight on the first day of the Battle of Gettysburg.

This dedication ceremony took place on August 21, 1909, in front of a crowd of 10,000 in the small Monroe County town of Union. Union had established Confederate reunions. The monument is located on the edge of the town. The base is native blue limestone. The granite pedestal is topped with a marble figure of a Confederate soldier. The monument took years to come to fruition, starting in 1900 with the laying of the cornerstone. The first Confederate reunion in the county was in 1894, when Gen. John Echols started a committee to raise money for a monument.

This photograph was taken at a reunion of the Society of Army of West Virginia in Wheeling on August 28, 1907. Joseph Trax is standing behind the "War Relic" banner, holding the cannon rammer and sporting a large flowing mustache. This trooper, formerly of the 2nd West Virginia Cavalry, had a cannon (Custer Cannon) cast from battlefield relics. The *Wheeling Intelligencer* said, "He had the cannon cast at the Fort Pitt works, Pittsburgh, and it is composed of bugles, shells, badges, sabres and relics from various battlefields from all parts of the country. Trax was an orderly under Custer during the civil war, and the cannon for him, while on it is engraved the shoulder straps of Custer, also flags, eagles and various other designs. In all, there are in its composition 118 relics of the Blue and Gray. The cannon has been exhibited at 24 national encampments, 24 reunions, 9 state encampments, and many other affairs." Trax took the 252-pound gun to many more reunions and encampments.

A major social event in Pendleton County was the Reunion of Civil War Veterans, which began in 1885 and continued for 35 years. These Confederate reunions were held in Franklin. This one, in 1919, included some of the few remaining Confederate veterans, along with veterans of World War I.

James Johnston Pettigrew, a Confederate general, was mortally wounded on July 14, 1863, at Falling Waters. He was taken across the Potomac to Edgewood Manor plantation, where he died on July 17. Edgewood Manor was built by Gen. Elisha Boyd in 1839. Shown here is the dedication of a monument to the general in 1918 by the North Carolina Historical Commission and the North Carolina Division, United Daughters of the Confederacy. The monument is located near Bunker Hill on US Route 11. (Courtesy Berkeley County Historical Society.)

This is the 4th West Virginia Infantry Monument dedication at Vicksburg, Mississippi, in November 1922. The likeness is of Maj. Arza M. Goodspeed, who was killed at Vicksburg. Besides this monument, the state of West Virginia erected four markers to identify the location of the 4th West Virginia Infantry. They include assault markers for May 19 and May 22, 1863. The monument and markers were made by the Sears Monument Company of Charleston, West Virginia. (Courtesy West Virginia State Archives.)

The dedication of Union Monument in Clarksburg took place on Decoration Day, May 30, 1908. The Wallace Circle Ladies of the GAR commissioned the monument. At that time, there were still many Union veterans in Harrison County. To be inclusive, the monument was dedicated to Harrison County soldiers that served in all wars from 1776 to 1907. The depicted soldier, though, is of the Civil War era. (Courtesy Harrison County Historical Society.)

A reunion of Sheridan Scouts was held in Middletown, Virginia, on November 9, 1909. This group, sometimes known as the Jessie Scouts, wore Confederate uniforms and served as spies. They carried messages and undertook secret missions and "extra dangerous duty." Of these scouts, which numbered around 40 during the war, only four remained for this reunion. They are, from left to right, Henry K. Chrisman, 8th New York Cavalry; Arch H. Rowand Jr., 1st West Virginia Cavalry; John Riley, 12th Pennsylvania Cavalry; and Joseph E. McCabe, 17th Pennsylvania Cavalry. Rowand was awarded the Medal of Honor for his service.

Shown here is a McNeill Ranger reunion. This partisan group was an effective unit during the war. The members held reunions in Moorefield. Some 30 years after the war, the Rangers invited their wartime foes, the Ringgold Cavalry, to a reunion in Moorefield. The old foes had a great time.

This is a Confederate reunion in Franklin. To the left, in front of the veterans, are a group of ladies in white dresses. They were known as the Dixie Girls, young ladies from Pendleton County that were honored at the reunions. Pendleton County had about 900 men that joined the Confederate army and about 300 men that signed up for the Union army.

These Taylor County Civil War veterans pose in front of the Baltimore & Ohio train station in downtown Grafton in the 1920s. The third person from the right, with a cane, is Robert L. Tallman. The Grafton GAR post is the Jesse Reno Post No. 7. In 1867, Grafton held a "Flower Strewing Day," later called Memorial Day, to honor those who served the community and country during the Civil War. Grafton has the honor of celebrating the longest continuous Memorial Day observance in the country.

This is a group of Clarksburg veterans at a Blue and Gray reunion. In this photograph, the men's names are identified by numbers: 1. ex-senator M.M. Neely; 2. Jacob M. Swartz, 6th West Virginia Infantry; 3. Solomon Day, 14th West Virginia Infantry; 4. A.J. Hartman, 20th Virginia Cavalry; 5. D.C. Louchery, 6th West Virginia Infantry; 6. William L. Keys, 80th Ohio Infantry; 7. David O. Morgan, 31st Virginia Infantry; and 8. William H. Ramsey, 10th West Virginia Infantry.

The Henry Kyd Douglas Camp of the Sons of Confederate Veterans met in Shepherdstown in the early 1900s. These Sons of Confederate Veterans dedicated the Confederate Memorial in Elmwood Cemetery, Shepherdstown, on September 18, 1937. There are 239 Confederate soldiers buried in Elmwood Cemetery, 114 of who are casualties of the Battle of Antietam. A second monument in Elmwood Cemetery is to the Confederate soldiers of Jefferson County. There are 535 names on that monument. (Courtesy Jefferson County Museum.)

This 1904 reenactment of the Battle of Antietam was conducted by the US Marine Corps. The man pointing is Gen. John A. LeJeune, the 13th commandant of the Marine Corps. The two seated veterans are Francis M. Jones (left), who served in the 62nd Virginia Infantry, and Frederick Fultz, who served in the 13th Maryland Infantry. Jones enlisted in Braxton County.

This Confederate reunion at Sweat Springs, a resort in Monroe County, took place around 1900. As the years passed, the reunions turned into homecomings or simply ceased, as the old veterans faded away. Development at Sweat Springs started in the 1700s, and it opened as a health resort in 1833. It continued until about the time of the Civil War. After the war, the resort reopened, operating until the crash of 1929. In 1941, the state purchased it as a tuberculosis sanitarium.

Shown here is the Silver Drum Corps, made up of veterans. Nothing would stir the memories of the old veterans as much as the music from their Civil War service. Many of the Grand Army of the Republic organizations had musicians. These are members of the Meade GAR Post No. 6 of Fairmont.

BIBLIOGRAPHY

Adjutant General, State of West Virginia. *Annual Report for the Year Ended December 31, 1864.* Charleston, WV: John F. M'Dermot, Public Printer, 1865. Adj 1. 1: 1864.

———. *Annual Report for the Year Ended December 31, 1865.* Charleston, WV: John Frew, Public Printer, 1866. Adj 1. 1: 1865.

Cohen, Stan. *The Civil War In West Virginia.* Pictorial Histories Publishing Company, 1995.

Curry, Richard O. *A House Divided: A Study of Statehood Politics and the Copperhead Movement in West Virginia.* Pittsburgh: University of Pittsburgh Press, 1964.

Ecelbarger, Gary L. *Frederick W. Lander: The Great Natural American Soldier.* Baton Rouge: Louisiana State University Press, 2001.

Greene, Israel. "The Capture of John Brown." *North American Review.* December 1885, University Press, 2000.

Lang, Theodore F. *Loyal West Virginia: From 1861 to 1865.* Baltimore: Deutsch Publishing Company, 1895.

Lesser, W. Hunter. *Rebels at the Gate: Lee and McClellan on the Front Line of a Nation Divided.* Naperville, IL: Sourcebooks, Inc., 2004.

Lowry, Terry and Cohen, Stan. *Images of the Civil War in West Virginia.* Missoula, MT: Pictorial Histories Publishing Company, 2000.

Matheny, H.E. *Wood County, West Virginia, in Civil War Times.* Parkersburg, WV: Trans-Allegheny Books, Inc., 1987.

Snell, Mark A. *West Virginia and the Civil War: Mountaineers Are Always Free.* Charleston, SC: History Press, 2011.

Toomey, Daniel Carroll. *The War Came By Train.* Baltimore: Baltimore & Ohio Railroad Museum, 2013.

CPSIA information can be obtained
at www.ICGtesting.com
Printed in the USA
LVHW010035070520
654940LV00018B/1332